Being a kid is hard. Sometimes you have big feelings. Other times you may have feelings you do not understand. It is OK to have your feelings. This book is to help you get your feelings out with a scribble.

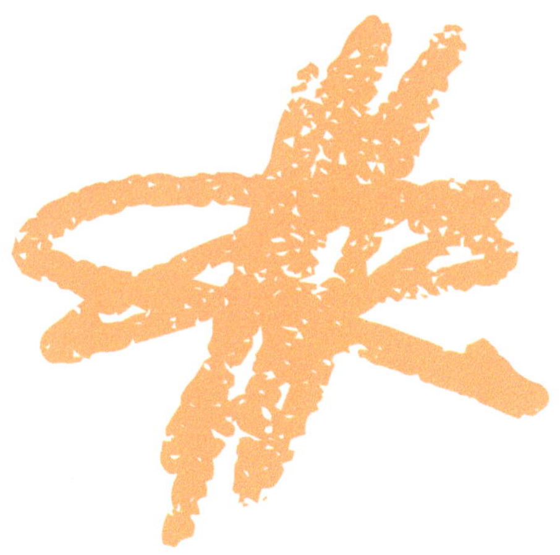

Scribble the color of your feeling on a circle.

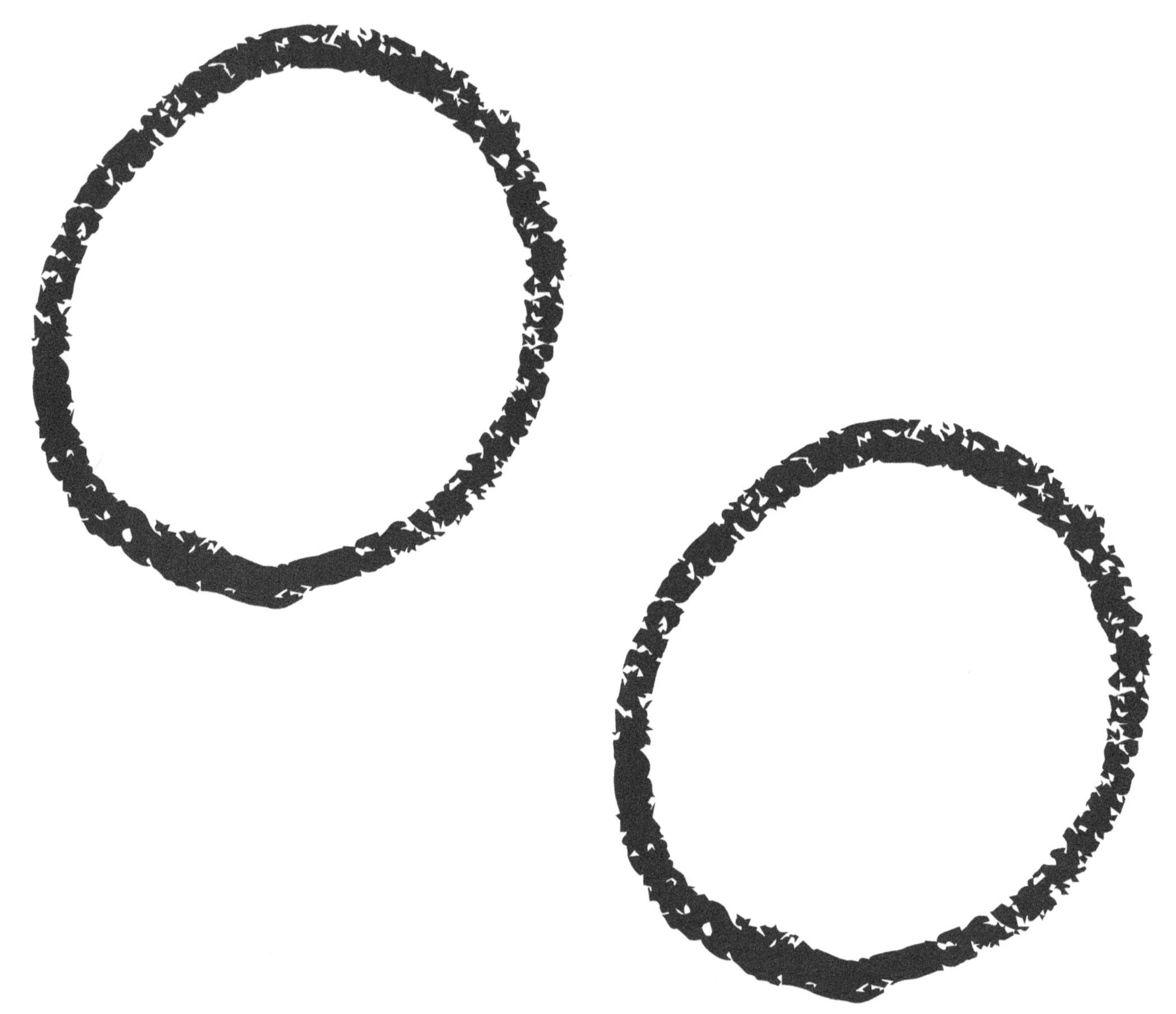

Scribble the color of your feeling around the circles.

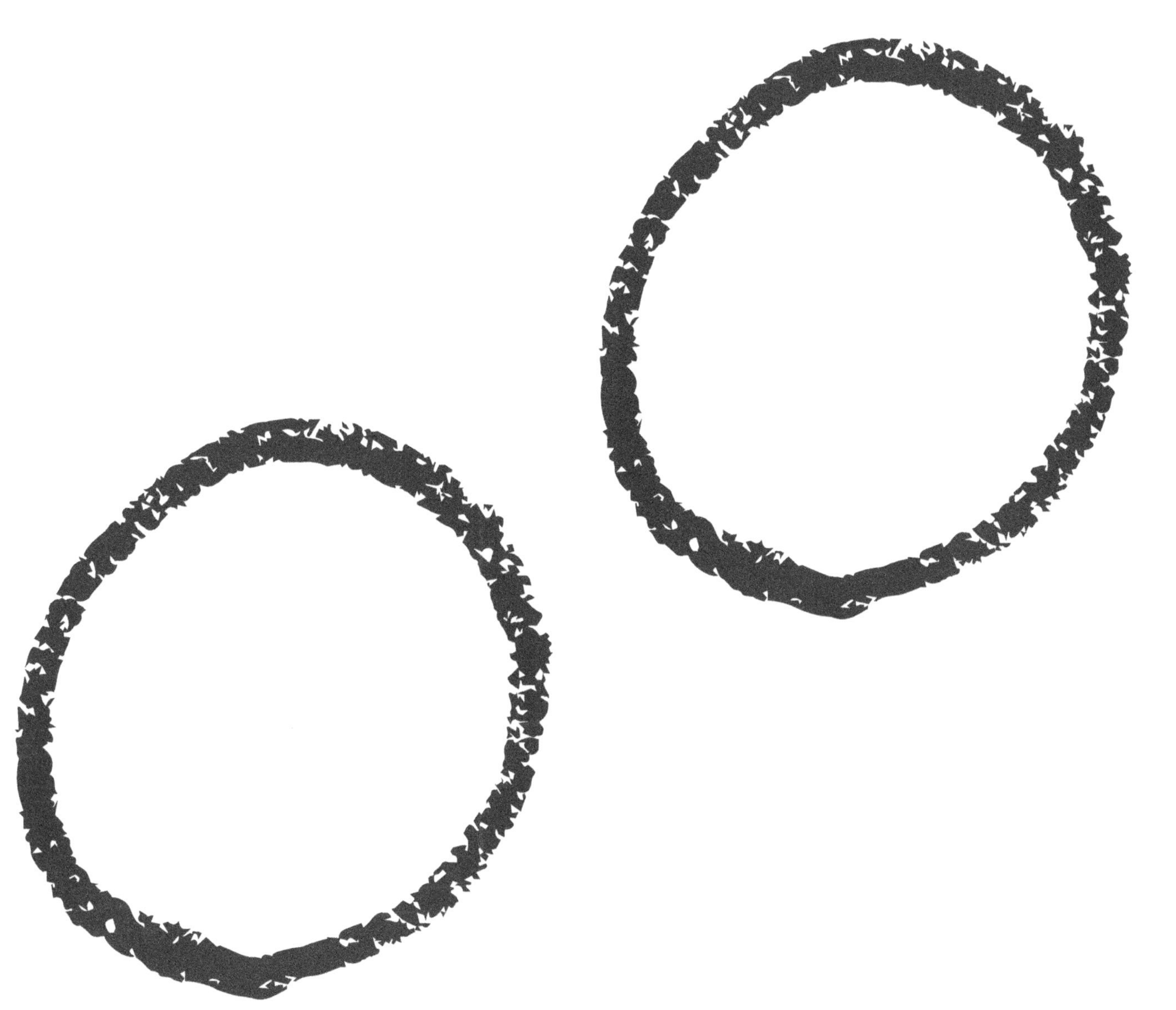

Scribble over each shape with a different color.

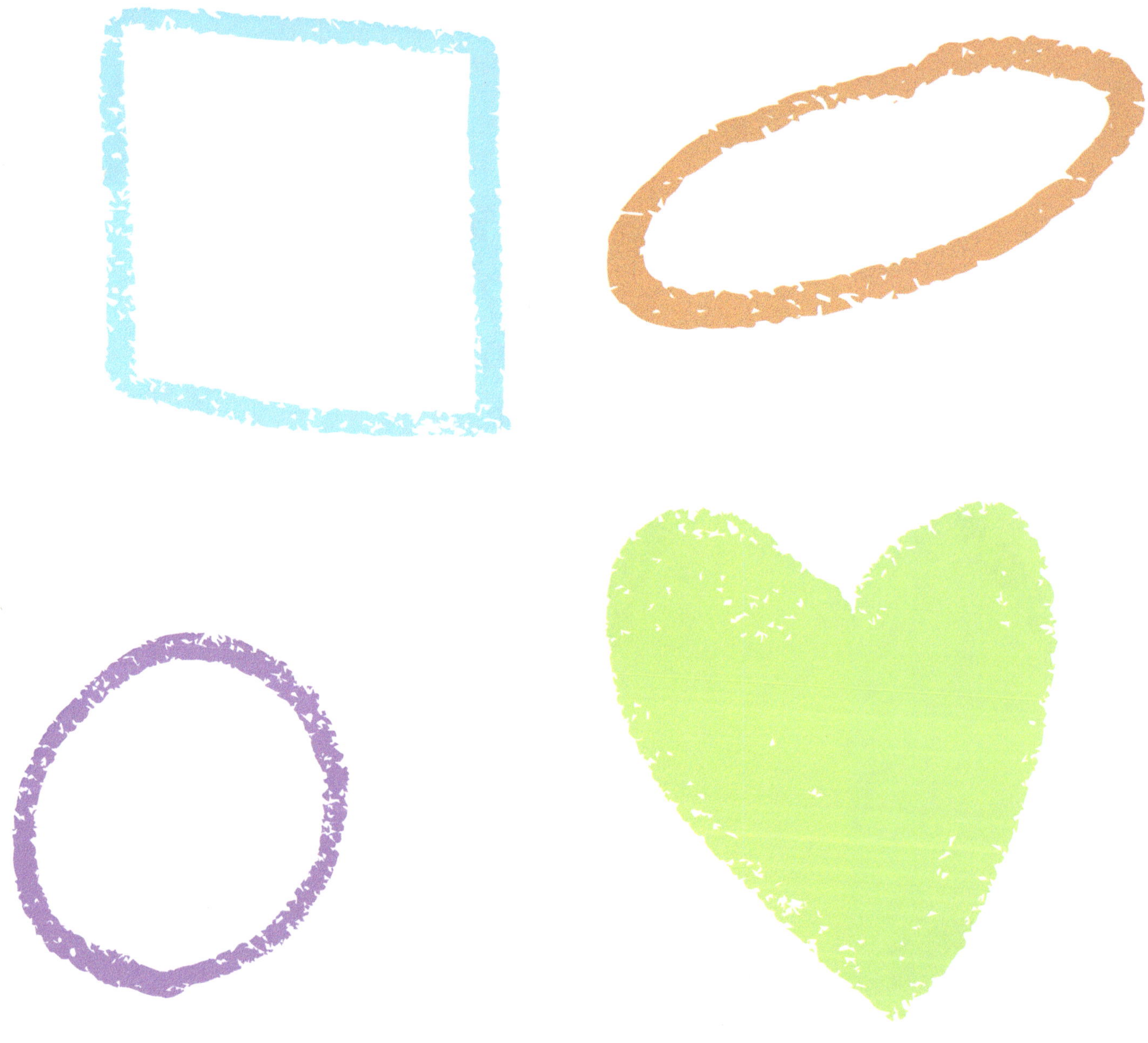

Scribble around each shape.

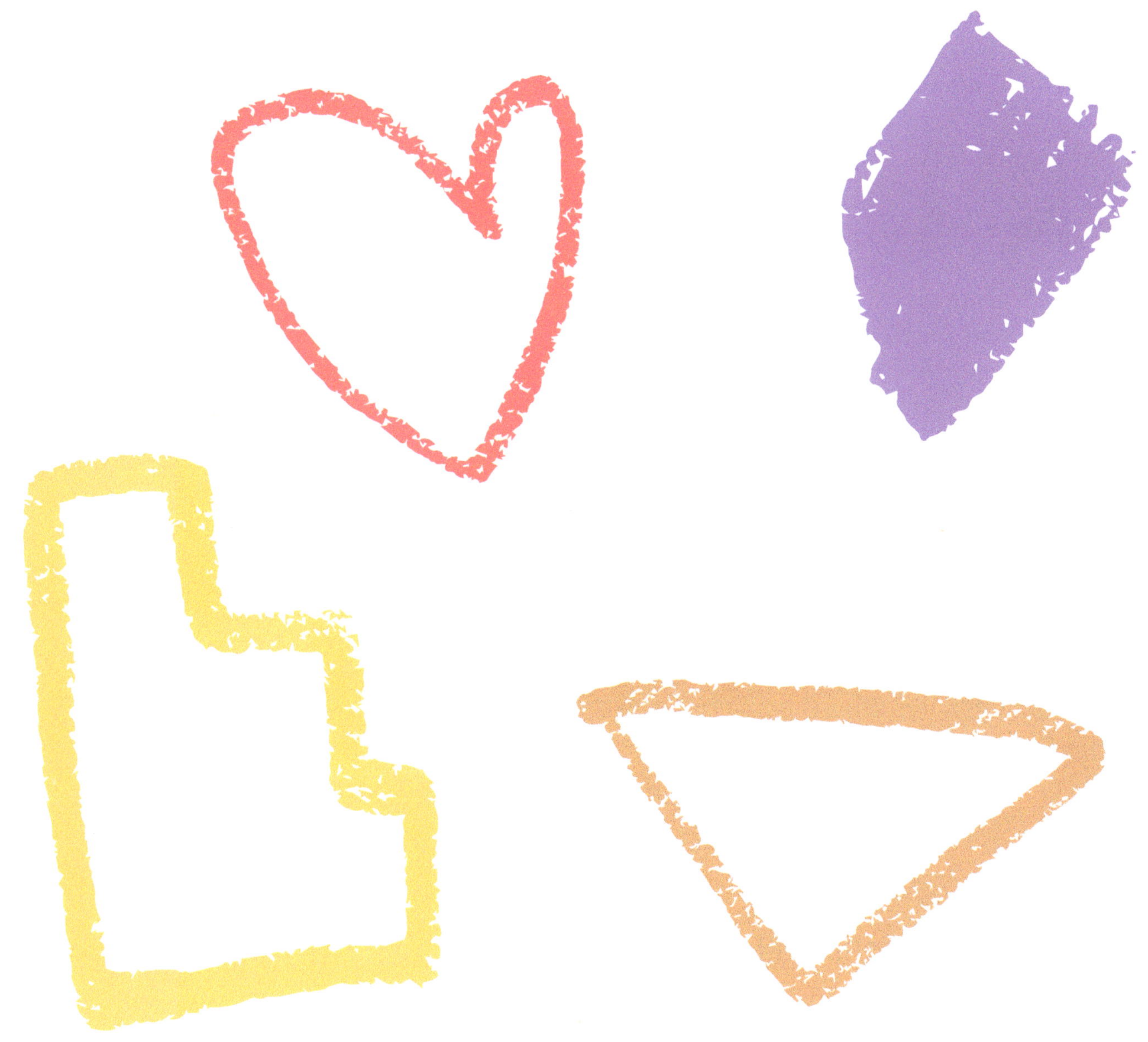

Scribble all over this page.

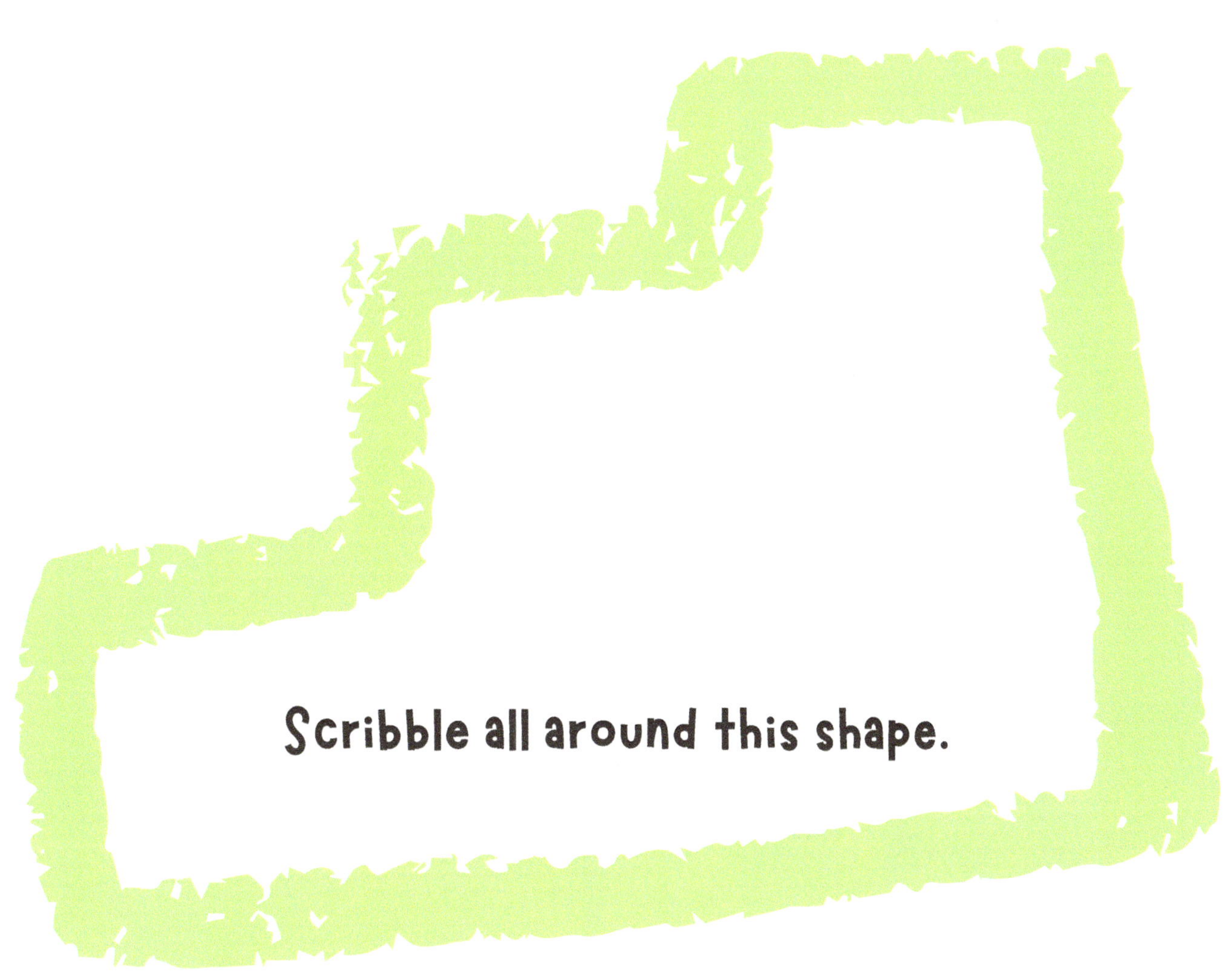

Scribble all around this shape.

Scribble your own spiral, loops, or curls.

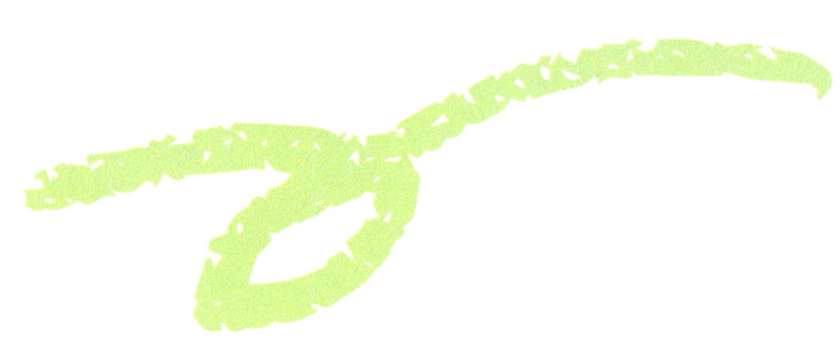

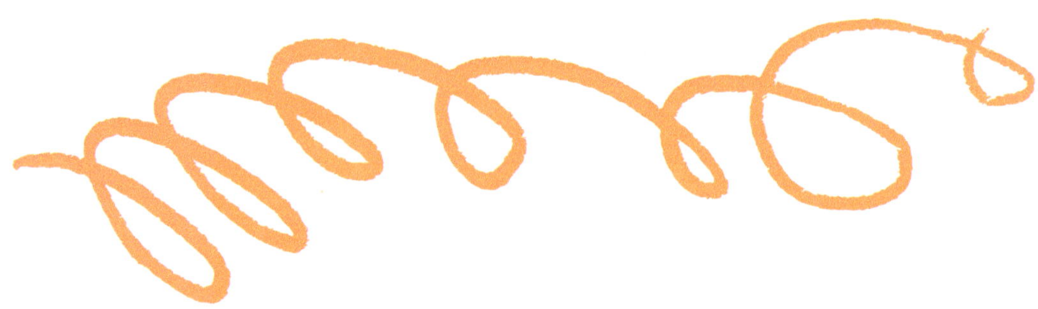

Scribble your own shapes.

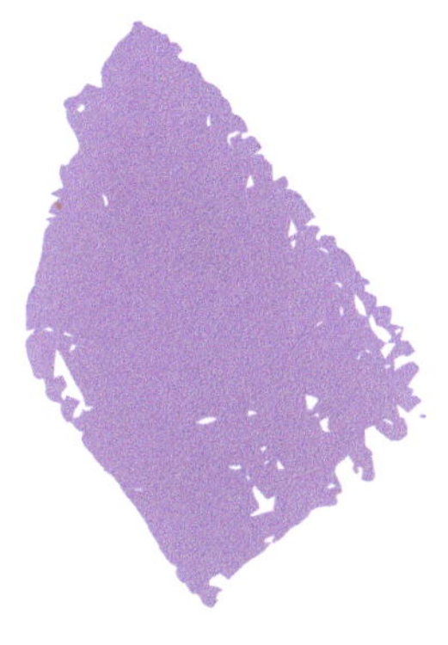

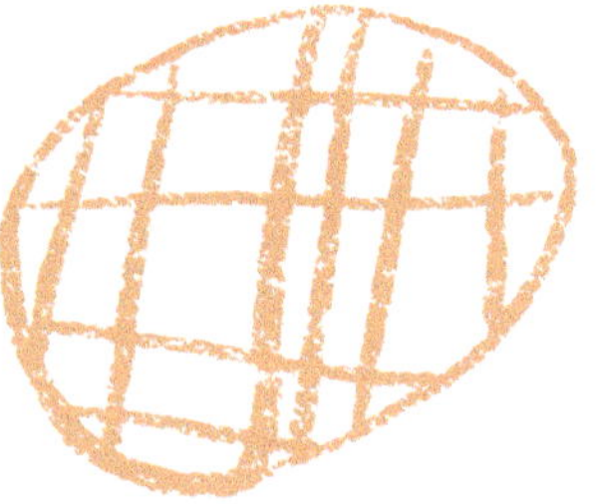

Scribble on the dots while you blow on them.

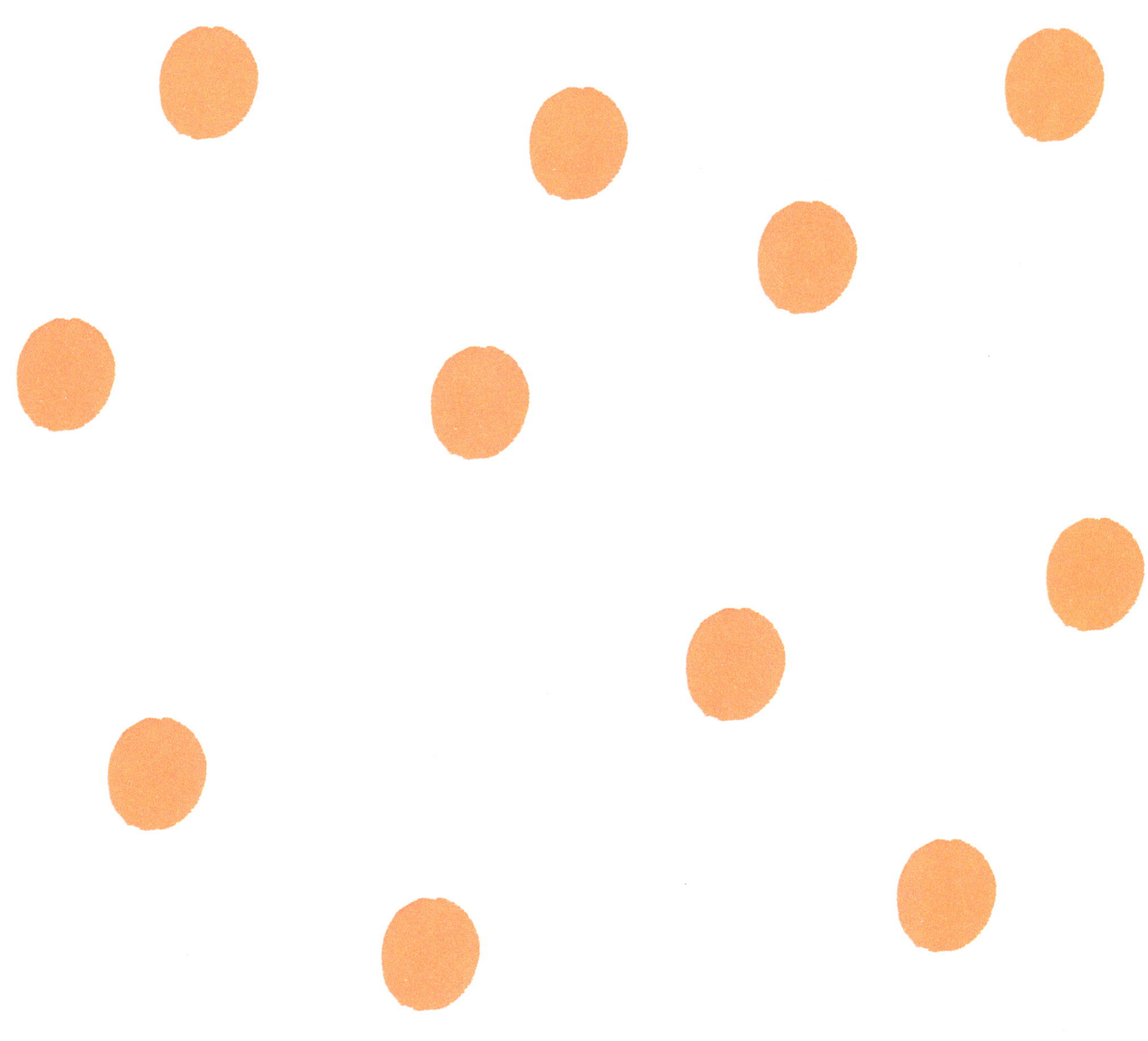

Scribble around the dots.

Scribble as hard as you can.

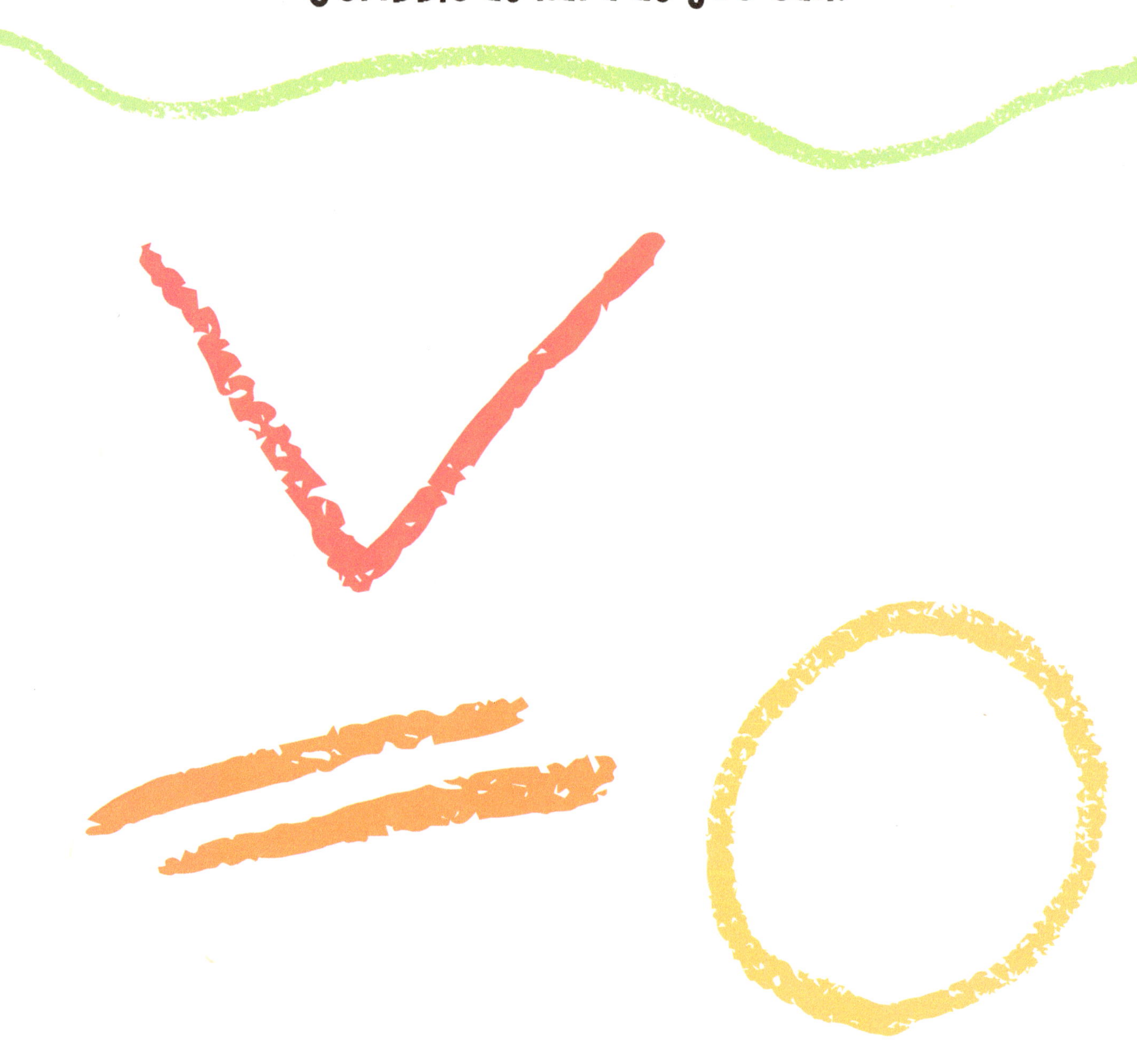

Scribble as hard as you can with both hands.

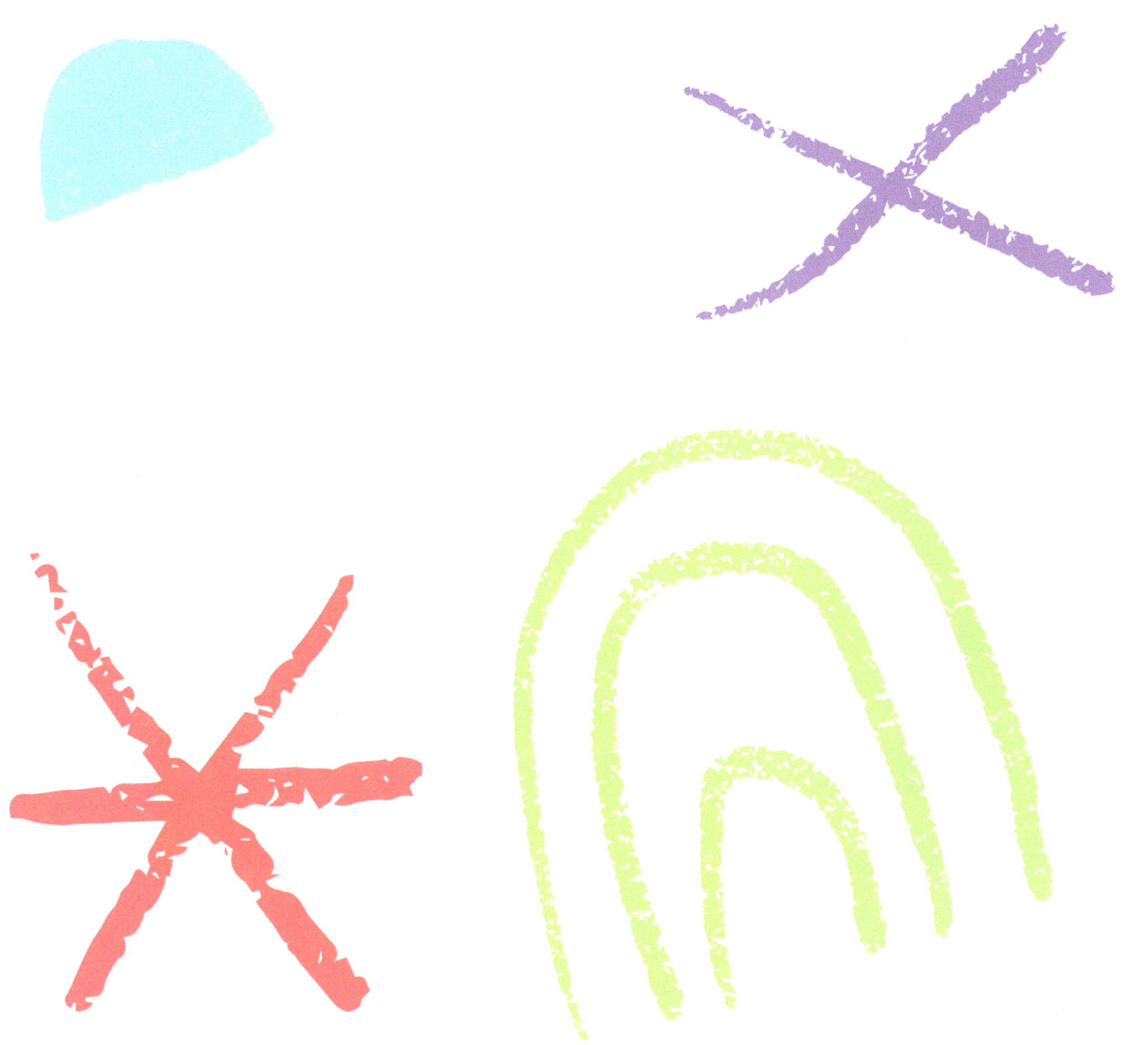

Scribble a face on the circle.

Scribble a face on the circle.

Scribble a face on the circle.

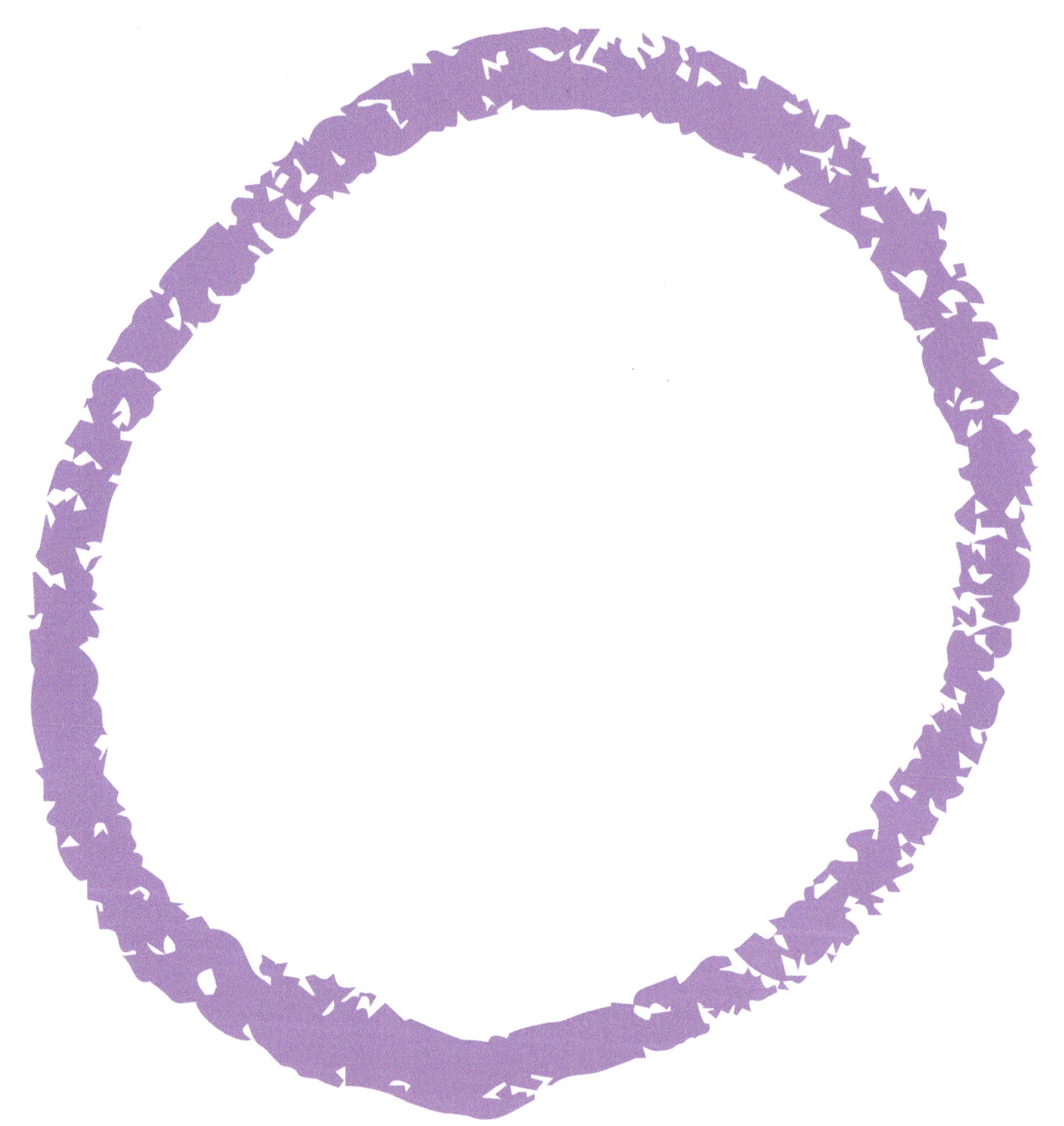

Scribble a face on the circle.

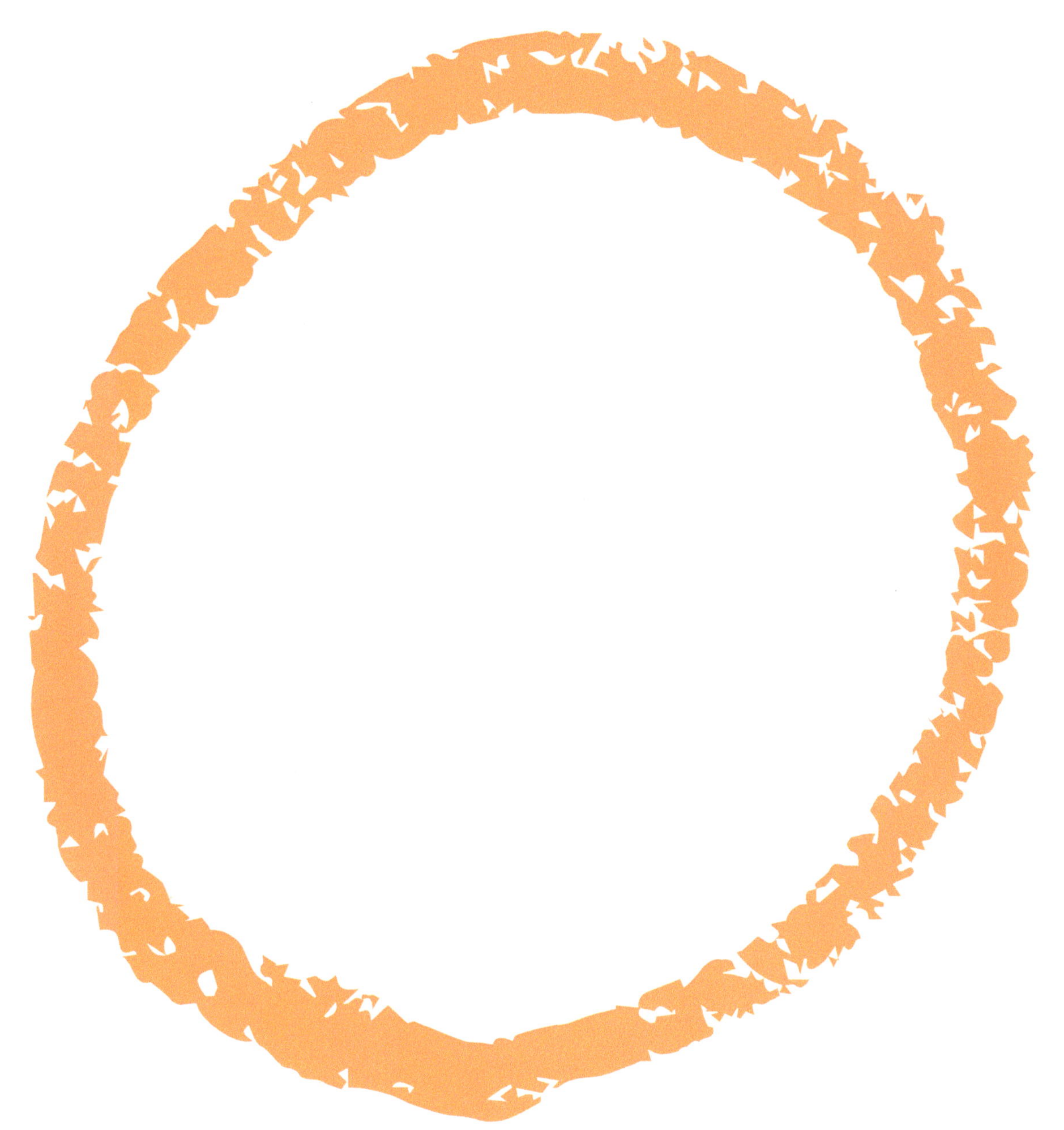

Scribble a face on the circle.

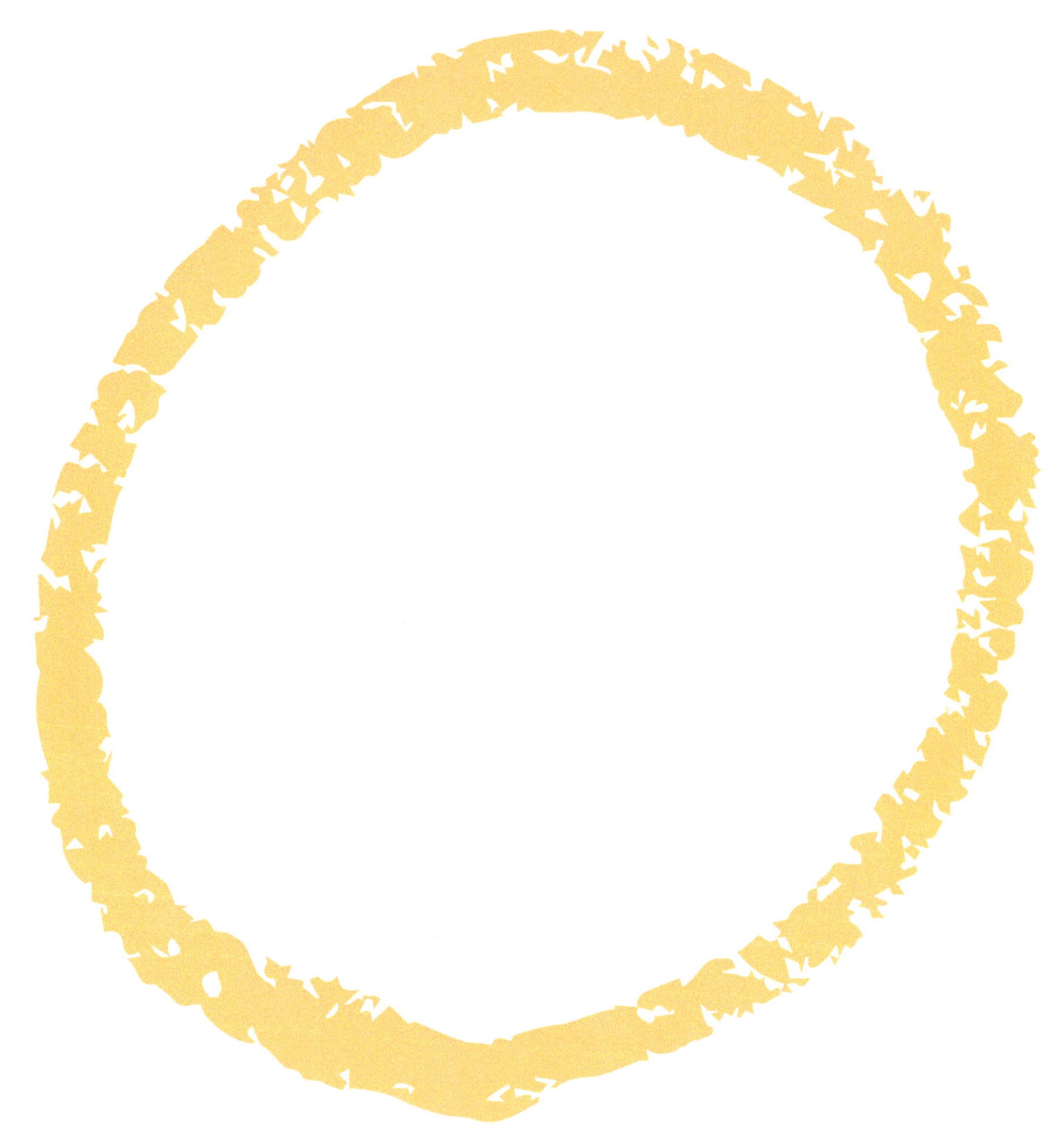

Scribble a face on the circle.

Scribble in all directions.

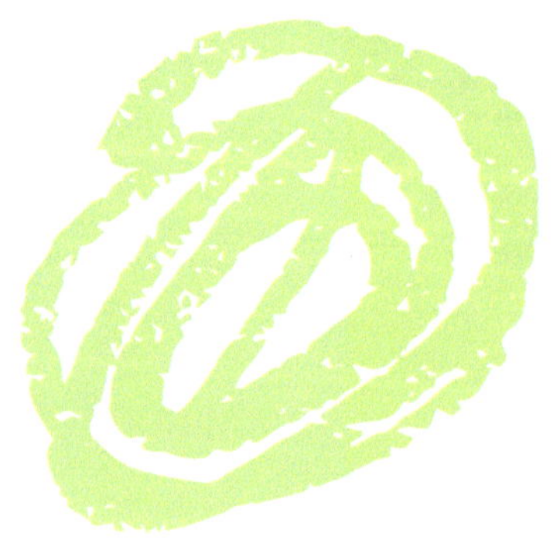

Scribble your own way.

Scribble as light as you can.

Scribble while you say a prayer.

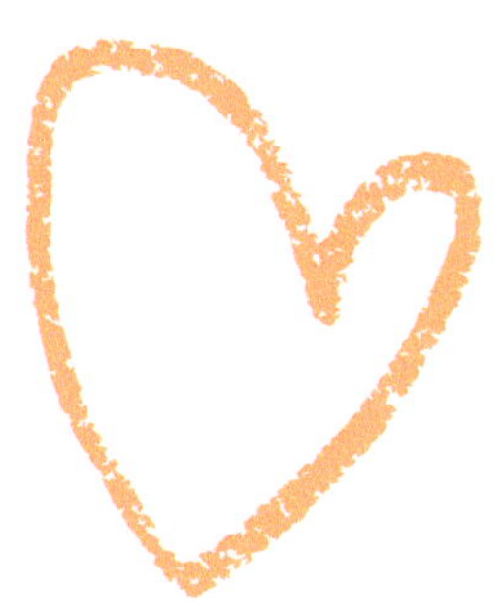

Scribble while counting to ten.

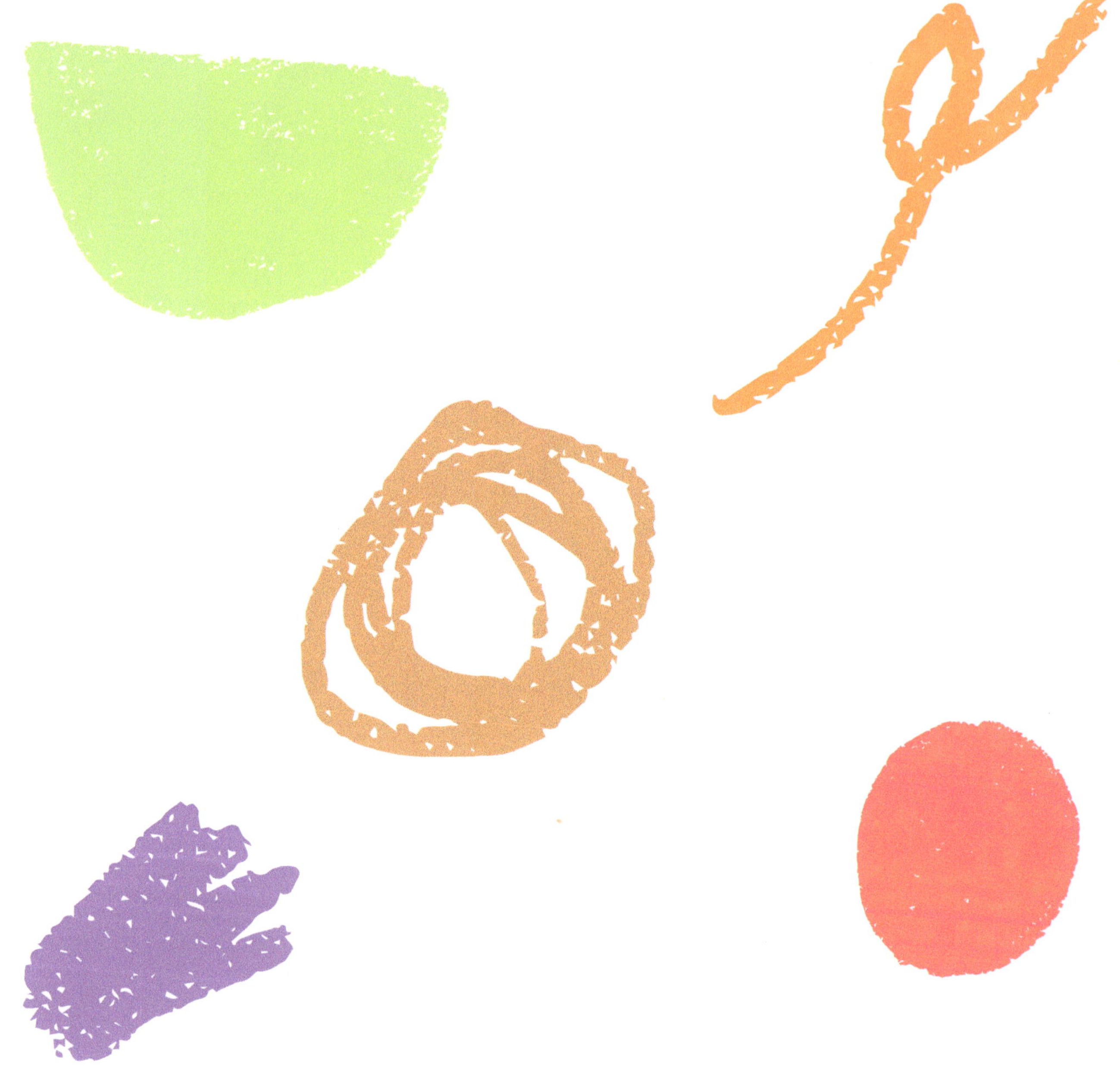

Scribble while singing your
favorite song.

Scribble while thinking about playing outside.

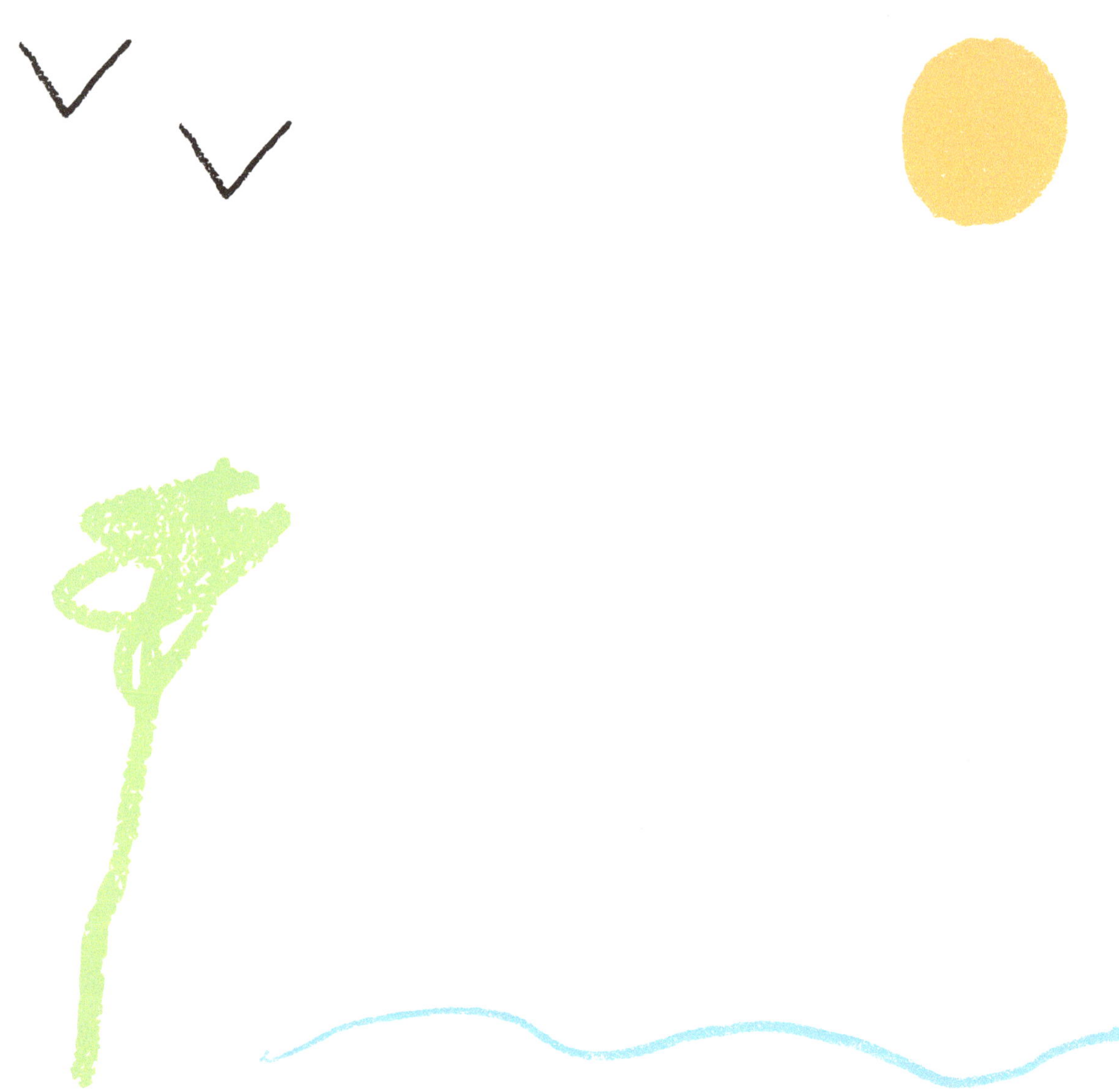

Scribble while your eyes are closed.

Scribble a note to your feelings.

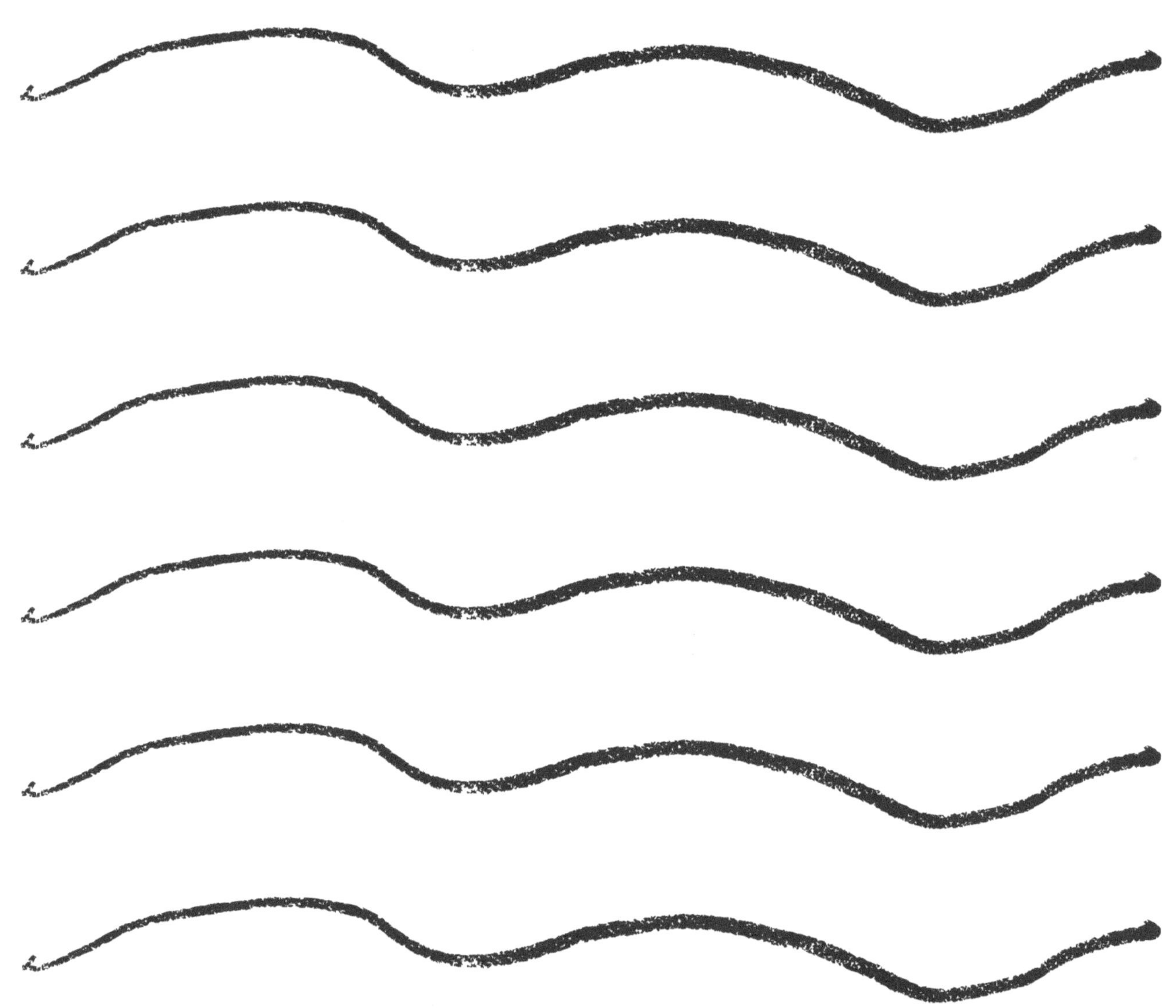

Scribble a note from your feelings.

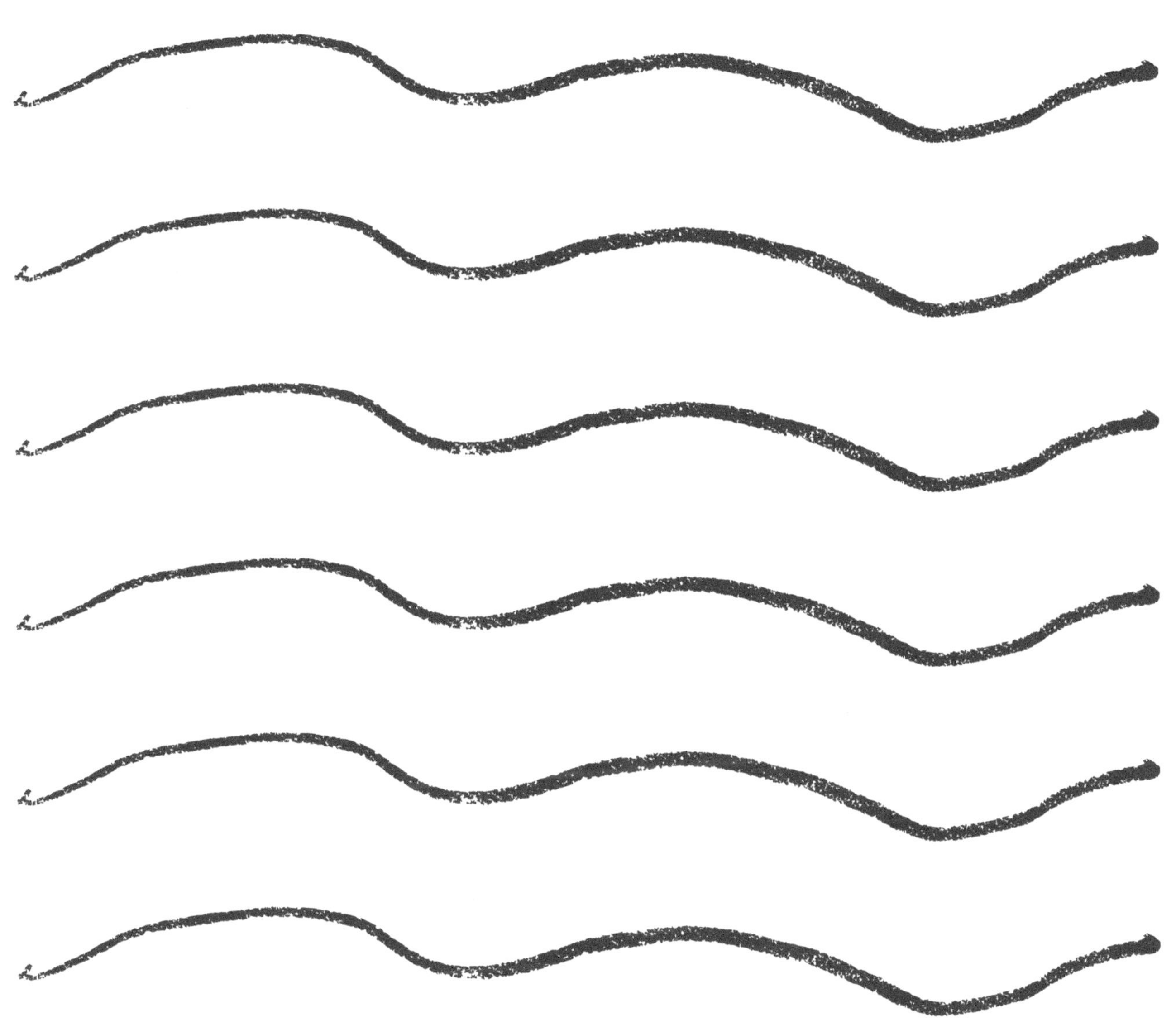

For Makenna because sometimes
you need to scribble.

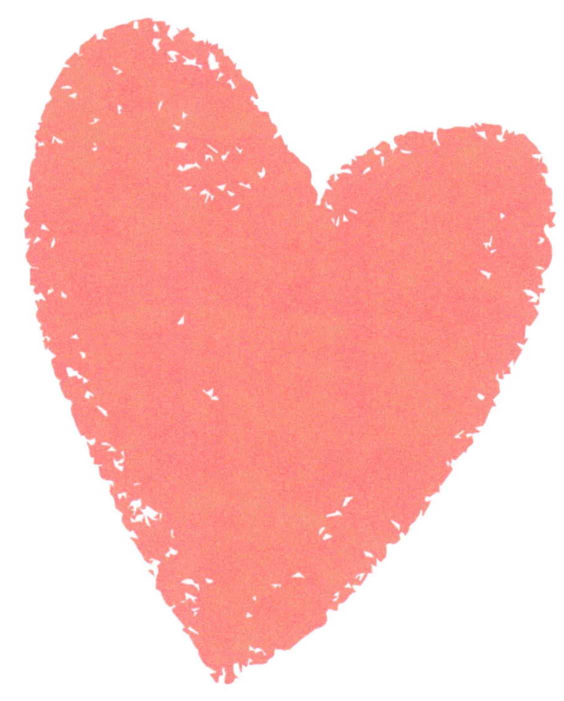

www.ingramcontent.com/pod-product-compliance
Lightning Source LLC
Chambersburg PA
CBHW040221110726
48005CB00019B/3105